A Colony of
Prairie Dogs

Heinemann Library
Chicago, Illinois

Richard and Louise Spilsbury

Customer Service 888-454-2279

Visit our website at www.heinemannlibrary.com

Designed by Heinemann Library
Photo research by Bill Broyles
Originated at Dot Gradations, UK
Printed in Hong Kong, China by Wing King Tong

08 07 06 05 04
10 9 8 7 6 5 4 3 2 1

Library of Congress Cataloging-in-Publication Data
Spilsbury, Louise.
  A colony of prairie dogs / Louise and Richard Spilsbury.
      p. cm. -- (Animal groups)
Includes bibliographical references and index.
  ISBN 1-4034-4693-8 (HC library binding) 1-4034-5415-9 (PB)
  1. Prairie dogs--Juvenile literature. I. Spilsbury, Richard, 1963-
II. Title. III. Series.
  QL737.R68S65 2004
  599.36'7--dc21
                           2003010346

Acknowledgments
The author and publishers are grateful to the following for permission to reproduce copyright material:
title page, icons, pp. 25, 31 Corbis; p. 4 M. P. Kahl/Photo Researchers, Inc.; pp. 5, 19 Wendy Shattil and Bob Rozinski/Oxford Scientific Films; p. 6 John Gerlach/DRK Photo; p. 7 Bob Gurr/DRK Photo; pp. 8, 17 W. Perry Conway/Corbis; p. 9 Jerry C. Ferrara/Photo Researchers, Inc.; pp. 10, 26, 27 Stephen J. Krasemann/DRK Photo; p. 11 Ken M. Highfill/Photo Researchers, Inc.; pp. 12, 14 Renee Lynn/Photo Rsearchers, Inc.; p. 13 Rod Planck/Photo Researchers, Inc.; p. 15 Kevin Schafer/Corbis; p. 16 Stephen G. Maka/DRK Photo; pp. 18, 21, 22, 24, 28 Tom and Pat Leeson/DRK Photo; p. 20 Martyn Colbeck/Oxford Scientific Films; p. 23 George D. Lepp/Corbis.

Cover photograph: W. Perry Conway/Corbis

The authors would like to dedicate this book to their own pups, Miles and Harriet.

The publisher would like to thank Dr. Steven W. Buskirk of the Department of Zoology and Physiology at the University of Wyoming for his comments in the preparation of this book.

Some words are shown in bold, **like this.** You can find out what they mean by looking in the glossary.

Contents

What Are Prairie Dogs?

Prairie dogs are small, chubby animals that commonly live in **burrows** on the **prairie**. Prairie dogs have brownish-tan hair and a round head with large eyes. They have short, five-toed feet with large claws, and a short tail. Male and female prairie dogs look very similar, but the male is slightly larger.

Prairie dogs are not dogs at all—they are a kind of **rodent**. Rodents are **mammals** with long **incisor** teeth. There are 2,016 different kinds of rodents in the world, ranging in size from just a few inches (6 centimeters) to over 4 feet (1.3 meters) long. Prairie dogs are small, burrowing rodents that are closely related to ground squirrels.

The black-tailed prairie dog gets its name because of the black tip on the end of its tail. Prairie dogs are 14 to 17 inches (36 to 43 centimeters) long—about the size of a guinea pig. They weigh 2 to 3 pounds (1 to 2 kilograms).

A dog's bark

Prairie dogs got their name because of their warning cry, which sounds a little like a dog's bark. The animals were named "little dogs" by Meriwether Lewis and William Clark during their exploration of North America in the early 1800s.

Groups of prairie dogs

There are five different **species**, or kinds, of prairie dogs: black-tailed, white-tailed, Gunnison's, Utah, and Mexican. Such things as hair color and where the different prairie dogs live define the different species. All prairie dogs are **social** animals that live in big groups. Large groups of prairie dogs are called **colonies.** In this book we will focus on the most common species: the black-tailed prairie dog.

This group of prairie dogs is just a small part of a larger colony.

5

What Is a Prairie Dog Colony Like?

A prairie dog **colony** might contain hundreds or even several thousand animals. Within the colony are a number of smaller family groups called **coteries**. A coterie is made up of about twelve animals. There is usually one adult male, four or five adult females that are closely related—sisters, mothers, or aunts—and their young, which are called **pups.** Some coteries contain twice this number, perhaps with two males.

Prairie dogs within a coterie share everything from food to chores. Members of a coterie work together and take turns to dig and mend **burrows** and look out for danger. Prairie dogs from different coteries do not usually mix with each other.

Multiple coteries and the burrows in which they live make up a colony.

6

Where Do Prairie Dogs Live?

Prairie dogs live in **prairies** in the United States, Canada, and Mexico. A prairie **habitat** is a **grassland** that is flat or has rolling hills. It is covered with tough, wild grasses and few trees.

Black-tailed prairie dogs are the most common and live from central Texas up into Canada. White-tailed prairie dogs live in Colorado, Utah, Wyoming, and Montana. The Gunnison's prairie dog lives where Utah, Colorado, Arizona, and New Mexico meet. The Mexican prairie dog lives only in certain parts of Mexico, and the Utah prairie dog is found only in central and southern Utah.

Prairies are areas where the soil is too poor or the weather too dry for trees or many other plants to grow.

7

What is a prairie dog town?

The place where a **colony** of prairie dogs lives is often called a **town.** A prairie dog town, like a human town, varies in size. It can range from one acre to hundreds of acres. A large town is divided into separate smaller areas in which several **coteries** live, a little like neighborhoods. A coterie from one area can see and hear nearby coteries, but they do not usually mix.

Cutting the grass

Prairie dogs bite off most of the tall plants around the town where their colony lives, keeping the grasses and other plants around the town short. This helps the prairie dogs get a better view of any predators that try to sneak up on the colony.

A prairie dog town is dotted with mounds of dirt and burrow entrances.

A coterie's territory

Each coterie of prairie dogs has its own **territory**. This is an area of land in which all the prairie dogs belonging to a coterie live, feed, and relax. Most of a prairie dog's travels are limited to its own territory. All the members of a coterie share **burrows** within their territory. They help each other keep prairie dogs from other coteries out of their territory.

Going underground

Each burrow within a coterie's territory is made up of tunnels that lead to several underground chambers, or rooms. Most burrows have at least two entrances, like having a front door and a back door. Some entrances may be covered with a piece of dirt and grass that can be removed quickly if necessary.

Members of a coterie dig out a burrow using their sharp, thick, black claws. This is hard work, so prairie dog coteries use the same burrows for many years.

9

Inside a prairie dog's burrow

The chambers inside a prairie dog's **burrow** are used for different things. The chamber nearest the surface is used for hiding if a **predator** is nearby. Farther underground there are toilet chambers, so that all the waste is kept in one place. There are deeper chambers that are kept dry. They are for sleeping or resting. Others, lined with grass, are where prairie dog babies are born and cared for.

The top of the burrow is raised into a cone-shaped mound. This is to stop water from flooding into the underground chambers during wet weather. It also makes a useful high point to look out for danger in the surrounding area.

Tunnels connecting the chambers go 3 to 6 feet (1 to 2 meters) below ground. They can be about 15 feet (5 meters) across.

This cutaway shows part of a typical prairie dog burrow.

10

On the **prairie** there are few bushes or other large plants to provide shade. Prairie dogs use their burrows to escape the sun on a hot day.

What Do Prairie Dogs Eat?

All prairie dogs are **herbivores**, or plant eaters. They sleep in their **burrows** at night and spend almost half their day feeding. Prairie dogs eat many different plant parts, including seeds, roots, leaves, flowers, and fruits. They occasionally eat insects such as beetles and grasshoppers.

Seasonal changes

For most kinds of prairie dog, food is in such short supply in winter that the only way they can survive is to **hibernate.** They go into a long sleep, deep in the burrow, and do not come out until spring. Black-tailed prairie dogs eat as much as they can in spring and summer to build up a layer of fat to help them through the winter. They spend several days at a time in their burrow during bad weather, but they may come out on sunny afternoons to find food.

Prairie dogs usually eat close to the safety of their burrow.

Eating plants

A prairie dog uses its **incisors** to chop down tall plants, break open the hard shells of seeds, and even strip bark from shrubs. The strong, grinding **molars** in the back of its mouth chew its food. Grass is difficult to **digest**. Prairie dogs have **bacteria** in their stomachs that help them digest. Their bodies have to digest their food in two steps to break it down.

A juicy diet

All animals need water, but prairie dogs do not need to drink water from ponds or puddles. They get most of the water they need from the moist, leafy plants they eat.

A prairie dog shows its teeth while yawning. Eating wears down a prairie dog's incisors. But like all **rodents**, their incisors keep growing their whole lives.

How Do Prairie Dogs Relax?

Each **coterie** in a prairie dog **colony** is a close and affectionate group. After the day's feeding and digging is done, prairie dogs relax together in different ways. On summer days, they retreat inside their **burrow** to escape the midday heat. In winter, they stay in their burrow longer, but come out to enjoy the sunshine on warmer days. While inside their burrow, prairie dogs doze, play, or **groom** each other.

Playtime

It is mostly the **pups** that play, but adults often play, too. When prairie dogs play, they pat and push each other, chase each other, and sometimes play fight. When prairie dogs play like this, it builds their muscles, sharpens their reactions, and strengthens friendships.

Prairie dog pups' play fighting can look quite rough, but they do not hurt each other.

Grooming

Grooming is an important part of a prairie dog colony's **social** life. One prairie dog will groom another by using its teeth to pick out dead skin, dirt, and tiny insects such as fleas from the other prairie dog's hair. Prairie dogs love to be groomed. They will often stretch and turn to be groomed in their favorite spots.

Prairie dogs groom to help keep each other's skin and hair clean, but that is not the only function of grooming. When animals in a group groom, they end up smelling alike because of the scent in their **saliva.** It is also a friendly thing to do which makes the animals feel closer to each other. These things all help the prairie dogs in a coterie feel more like a team.

Prairie dogs sit very still while they are being groomed.

How Do Prairie Dogs Care for Their Young?

Prairie dogs are able to **breed,** or have babies, when they are about two years old. An adult male usually breeds with all the adult females in his coterie. Prairie dogs **mate** from March to April, and the babies are born about a month later.

Prairie dogs only have one **litter** of **pups** each year. A mother prairie dog usually has between four and six babies in a litter. She gets a nesting chamber ready for the babies before they are born. She carries grass down into a room in the **burrow** to make a warm and soft bed for them.

 This female prairie dog is pregnant. She is setting up a nest chamber where she will give birth and care for her babies.

Young prairie dogs

Prairie dog pups are completely helpless when they are born. They only weigh about half an ounce (15 grams) each—the weight of a tablespoon of sugar. They have no hair to keep them warm, and their eyes are closed for the first few weeks, so they cannot see. They cannot move around, and they rely on their mother for everything.

A mother prairie dog is very protective of her young. She keeps them safe in the burrow until they are six or seven weeks old. Like all **mammals**, the first food the pups take in is milk from their mother's body. This is called **suckling**. The milk is the only food the pups need in their first weeks of life. It also provides the water they need.

A pup's eyes open after two weeks, and its hair begins to grow after about three weeks.

When do pups leave the burrow?

By the time prairie dog **pups** are six or seven weeks old, they are alert and ready to come out of the **burrow**. At this time they stop **suckling**, and the mothers' milk supply dries up. The pups begin to eat grass and other plant foods, like other prairie dogs in the **coterie**.

Spring fever

There is an important reason why prairie dog pups, like many animals, are born in the spring. When the pups leave the burrow in May or June, there are lots of young, green grasses and flowers for them to eat. It is important for them to eat a lot and grow fat so that they can survive their first winter.

These prairie dog pups are coming out of the burrow into daylight for the first time.

Babysitters

A big advantage of living in a group is that the adults can help to look after each other's young. In a coterie of prairie dogs, adult males and females watch out for each other's babies when they emerge from the burrow. Sometimes, young pups follow someone else's mother. They may even end up sleeping in her burrow!

Growing up

Young prairie dogs need extra care when they first leave the burrow. It takes them a while to learn the dangers of the **prairie** and when they need to run to safety. As they grow up, pups learn to recognize warning calls and good places to eat. They get to know all the other members of their coterie. Prairie dogs are fully grown by October or November.

Adults from a coterie watch over young prairie dogs while they play and feed.

When prairie dogs are out of their **burrows**, they **communicate** with each other all the time. Prairie dogs bark to signal danger or scare off an intruder. They scream when scared, snarl in a fight, and call out to tell others where their **territory** is. Scientists think prairie dogs have one of the most advanced languages of any animals studied.

On guard

While a **coterie** of prairie dogs eats, at least one prairie dog stands guard on the top of a burrow mound. If it spots danger, it barks a warning to others. Then they all dive into their burrows. The guard, called a **sentry**, stays in the chamber nearest the surface so it can tell when the **predator** has moved away. The sentry gives a special call, known as the jump-yip, when it is safe for everyone to come back out.

The jump-yip is a two-part call that sounds like "Yahoo!"

What do they say?

Prairie dogs can make different sounds to identify different predators. For example, they make one kind of call to warn of an attacking bird, and a different call for a predator that walks on land. Some scientists think they can even tell the difference between people with guns and those without.

A hello kiss

Prairie dogs also communicate using touch and scent. When two prairie dogs meet, they crawl toward each other, open their mouths and touch teeth. This is called the kiss, because that is exactly what it looks like! Prairie dogs kiss to find out whether they are from the same coterie. If they are, the two animals usually **groom** each other's fur. If the visitor is not from the same coterie, it will be chased off.

Prairie dogs kiss and hug as a way of greeting each other.

Tail movements

Prairie dogs might also pass each other messages through body movements. Signals are often given using the tail. For example, a tail up seems to mean that a prairie dog is uneasy and is checking something out. It tells others to be alert. A tail sticking out seems to signal that the prairie dog is concentrating on something, such as eating.

Communication and the colony

Communication is a very important part of life in a **colony.** Even though different **coteries** do not mix, the colony is linked by communication. For example, when a prairie dog from one coterie makes a series of warning yips, members of other coteries hear it. They repeat the message and pass it on—until the news has spread throughout the whole colony!

A prairie dog's tail is 3 to 4 inches (8 to 10 centimeters) long. Its length helps make tail movements clear to other prairie dogs, even at a distance.

Do Prairie Dogs Fight?

As in any group, there are sometimes conflicts between prairie dogs in a coterie. These are usually sorted out through harmless scuffles. Most of the time, prairie dogs within a coterie are gentle toward each other.

The true fights that happen are usually between male prairie dogs from different coteries. They will fight if one tries to take over another's **burrow.** At first, the burrow owner sits outside its hole and barks continuously to warn off the intruder. This tells the intruder to move on or prepare to fight. This is usually enough to scare off the intruder. If these warnings do not work, the two animals fight, sometimes to the death.

In a fight, prairie dogs try to injure each other using their sharp claws and teeth.

The **coteries** in a prairie dog **colony** change every year. While most of the females in a coterie remain there most of their lives, the males may move on or be replaced by other males each spring.

Young male prairie dogs usually leave the coterie in which they were born when they are about a year old. They try to join or take control of a nearby coterie in the **town.** Others have to travel farther away and set up their own coteries with a female from another coterie. Many young prairie dogs die when they leave the safety of their coteries.

Young male prairie dogs may have trouble joining or taking over a coterie. Many are chased away and forced to live on the edges of the colony's town.

Changing the prairie

It is not only the coteries in a colony that change. Prairie dogs also change the way the area around their town looks. As they dig and extend their **burrows**, they loosen the soil. This, plus the fact that they cut down taller plants, means that other grasses and wildflowers are able to grow in the **habitat**. Their droppings enrich the soil and help a wider range of plants to grow there.

Guests in the burrow

Rabbits, mice, snakes, toads, salamanders, turtles, and many beetles make their homes in a prairie dog burrow. If rattlesnakes hibernate in their burrows in winter, prairie dogs seal up the tunnels and dig new ones. If they don't, the rattlesnakes may eat the pups in the burrow.

Burrowing owls move into abandoned burrows and live among prairie dog colonies.

What Dangers Does a Colony Face?

The prairie dogs in any **colony** face all sorts of dangers. They have many **predators**, or animals that try to catch and eat them. These include badgers, coyotes, weasels, eagles, hawks, rattlesnakes, and the swift fox.

Dangerous fleas

A disease called plague has wiped out many prairie dog colonies. Infected fleas pass on the disease when they bite a prairie dog. The disease can spread through a colony very quickly, killing many prairie dogs at a time.

Badgers may try to catch a prairie dog by rushing into a colony quick enough to get one before it runs down a burrow. Or, badgers dig into burrows to catch prairie dogs while they are sleeping.

How do prairie dogs escape predators?

Prairie dogs rely on good hearing, sharp eyesight, and quick reactions to escape predators. Prairie dogs are also helped by **camouflage.** Their hair color is similar to the ground in which they live, making it harder for predators to see them. The network of tunnels also helps them escape. When a predator such as a weasel crawls into a **burrow**, prairie dogs can plug up the tunnel with dirt and grass. This gives them enough time to escape through other tunnels.

The prairie dog's best protection is other prairie dogs looking out for danger. This is one of the advantages of living in a colony.

27

How do people harm prairie dogs?

One of the biggest threats to prairie dogs is people. People have taken over huge areas of the **prairie** for building and farming. Farmers, ranchers, and builders kill prairie dogs because their **burrows** make land difficult for farming or building. In some places, millions of prairie dogs are shot each year for sport. Because of people, the number of prairie dogs is decreasing all the time.

Prairie dog benefits

Prairie dogs are an important and useful animal. Their digging brings air into the soil to keep it healthy and their droppings **fertilize** it to help plants grow. Large **herbivores**, such as bison and antelope, come to feed on the plants around prairie dog **towns**. Other animals rely on prairie dogs as their food. Some of these include **endangered species** such as the black-footed ferret.

Some people think prairie dogs take too much prairie grass from other herbivores. Other people think these different animals can live side by side.

Prairie Dog Facts

Where do prairie dogs live?

This map shows where wild prairie dogs live today.

Key
- Black-tailed prairie dog
- White-tailed prairie dog
- Utah prairie dog
- Gunnison's prairie dog
- Mexican prairie dog

CANADA

UNITED STATES

Atlantic Ocean

Pacific Ocean

MEXICO

What was the biggest colony?

In the past, prairie dog **colonies** were much larger than they are today. The biggest colony recorded was found in Texas in 1900. It was about 100 miles (161 kilometers) wide and 250 miles (402 kilometers) long. It was home to about 400 million prairie dogs.

How fast can prairie dogs run?

Prairie dogs react very quickly to danger. When alarmed, they can run 35 miles (56 kilometers) per hour over short distances to get to the safety of a burrow.

How long do prairie dogs live?

Most prairie dogs live only three to five years in the wild. Males tend to have a shorter life span than females, because males get killed or badly injured in fights.

How many prairie dogs are left?

The number of black-tailed prairie dogs is now only about one percent of what it was in the past. The black-tailed prairie dog species is considered threatened. This means that without protection, it may die out completely.

29

Glossary

bacteria tiny living things that can usually be seen only through a microscope

breed have babies

burrow hole or tunnel dug by an animal for shelter

camouflage colors and patterns that help an animal blend in with its background

colony group of living things of one kind living together

coterie family group of prairie dogs

communicate pass on information to another

digest break down food inside a body so that it can be absorbed

endangered in danger of dying out

grassland area of land that is mainly covered with grass

groom when one animal cleans bits of dirt, dead skin, or insects from the hair of another animal

habitat place where an animal or plant lives

herbivore animal that eats mainly plants

hibernate go into a long and very deep sleep during cold weather

incisors four front teeth in an animal's mouth, two on the top and two on the bottom, used to bite into food

litter young animals produced by an animal at one time

mammal hairy, warm-blooded animal that feeds its young with milk from the mother's body

mate joining of a male and female of the same species to create young

molars flat-topped teeth at the back of an animal's mouth used to grind food

prairie areas of grassland with few trees

predator animal that hunts other animals for food

pup newborn or young prairie dog

rodent mammal that has long incisor teeth that grow throughout its life

saliva liquid made in the mouth

sentry one who serves as a lookout

social living in a group

species group of living things that are alike in many ways and can mate to produce young

suckling drinking milk from a mother's body

territory particular area that a group of animals claims as its own

town area that includes all the burrows that belong to one prairie dog colony

More Books to Read

Johnson, Rebecca L. *A Walk in the Prairie*. Minneapolis: Lerner, 2001.

Kline, Trish. *Prairie Dog's Burrow*. Norwalk, Conn.: Soundprints, 2002.

Redmond, Shirley-Raye. *Lewis and Clark: A Prairie Dog for the President*. New York: Random House, 2003.

Staub, Frank. *Prairie Dogs*. Minneapolis: Lerner, 1998.

Unwin, Mike. *The Life Cycle of Mammals*. Chicago: Heinemann, 2003.

An older reader can help you with these books:

Patent, Dorothy Hinshaw. *Life in a Grassland*. Minneapolis: Lerner, 2002.

Robinson, W. Wright. *How Mammals Build Their Amazing Homes*. Farmington Hills, Mich.: Gale Group, 1999.

Index